Differentiating Professional Development:
The Principal's Role

by
Michelle Pedigo

National Middle School Association
Westerville, Ohio

National Middle School Association
4151 Executive Parkway, Suite 300
Westerville, OH 43081
1-800-528-NMSA

Sue Swaim, Executive Director
Jeff Ward, Associate Executive Director
April Tibbles, Director of Publications
Sara Hemphill, Production Manager
Edward Brazee, Editor, Professional Publications
John Lounsbury, Consulting Editor, Professional Publications
Mary Mitchell, Designer, Editorial Assistant
Marcia Meade-Hurst, Senior Publications Representative
Mark Shumaker, Cover Design

ISBN: 1-56090-138-1

Contents

Preface

Schools are under the gun to raise student achievement, meet standards, and be accountable for improving the achievement of *all* students. In desperation, schools have resorted to threats, bribes, and academic pep rallies complete with cheers and slogans as a means of motivating students to do their best on upcoming tests. A more valid and professional, although time-consuming way to reach the accountability goals, however, is to ratchet up the skills of the faculty. Teachers, who work directly and continuously with students in the classroom are, after all, the only ones who can bring about meaningful improvement in students' achievement. Professional development, the best means for improving the performance of faculty members, is a major responsibility of the school principal.

Too often professional development has meant a particular program or new strategy was identified and then "taught" to the entire faculty. But rarely was such a program "taken" by teachers and implemented in the classroom. This resource provides guidance in developing different ways to conduct professional development. It is based on the simple and very valid premise that teachers, like their students, are different. Although there is still a place for faculty-wide professional development, to effect meaningful changes in the performance of teachers, principals need to recognize and act on the fact that the needs and learning styles of teachers are varied and, therefore, professional development activities must be likewise.

The author, Michelle Pedigo, former principal of Barren County (Kentucky) Middle School, was the 2001 National Principal of the Year. Her thoughts and suggestions found in this resource, therefore, have a proven, field-based validity. Principals and other middle level leaders are encouraged to capitalize on the advice contained here as they work to successfully improve students' achievement. — JHL

TOPIC 1

Why Hasn't Professional Development Succeeded?

For many years now, we have funded various professional development opportunities for teachers. We have "in-serviced" them. We have sent them off to staff development. We have checked off dutifully the days they attended. All the while, we thought we were doing the right thing to create change in teacher pedagogy so that each and every student could be successful according to state standards, and so that our schools can accomplish "adequate yearly progress" according to the recently instituted federal assessment and accountability system. Alas, after all this work, a little change may have occurred, but not nearly enough. Why? Someone once said regarding professional development, "Our focus should be learning about what we do for a living every day – not just doing *something* with students."

This is an issue of professionalism, and building professionalism within a staff is crucial to achieving sustained school reform. Teachers are always asked to think about the students they serve, yet rarely are they expected to speak about themselves. They should be thinking about their own learning all the time. How can we, as educational leaders, help teachers to see that their own learning can produce higher student results?

For starters, we cannot treat them all alike. Teachers are like students. They all learn at different rates, in different ways, and at different times. Assuming that since they are adults they learn the same way can be likened to doctors' telling patients to take two aspirin, no matter what the symptoms. We would not expect physicians to practice in this manner; neither then should we expect professional development to be the same for all teachers.

They aren't all alike

I thought Becky Moon did not like anyone – students, teachers, parents, and especially administrators. When I first met Becky, I was beginning as a vice-principal at Barren County Middle School. Becky was a veteran seventh grade teacher. Fresh from the classroom, I wasn't used to dealing with teachers as an administrator yet, but I did naïvely think that most of them would believe in what I believed, because I had been selected as their administrator. Becky taught me differently. At that time, she seldom if ever smiled and actually prided herself in putting fear into her students to coerce them to behave. When I walked into her classroom during a "building walk-through," she seemed very nervous, but she had her troops "under control." They were quiet, working in their seats as she patrolled the aisles, arms folded, scanning answers to the questions at the end of the chapter that the students were looking up. Sometimes, she just walked back and forth in front of the classroom with somewhat of a scowl, just to reinforce that she was in charge. Becky thought a quiet classroom was the goal, and she accomplished that.

Then there were the high-flying teachers at Barren County Middle School – those who thirsted for every new idea they could find to better serve their students. There were those who wanted to attend the national conference in their subject area or the National Middle School Association conference every year. There were teachers who knocked on my door with a flyer in hand. "I just got this brochure on coopera-tive learning strategies. May I attend this workshop?" they would plead. These teachers were very adept in their craft. They understood multiple intelligences and implemented varied activities with rigor. They led their teams in discussions on integrated teaching, and they read professional books to hone their craft.

Beth Thompson was one of these teachers. She had always been a leader in our school and understood quality teaching and learning. She was also a big part of Becky Moon's professional growth. When I set the expectation for a change in teacher behavior, Beth would "hold Becky's hand" and help her get there. Beth understood that Becky could do it, with a little hand holding, and she brought her along every time. Becky had never even turned her computer on when we introduced electronic gradebook and attendance, so Beth literally sat by her the first time she entered attendance and grades.

As a middle level principal, I knew Beth was a high flyer, yet I still had to expect Beth to improve, and I needed to know what improvement area she had chosen. For middle level educators, a big step in professional growth is to accept and truly believe that each and every child can learn and perform at high levels. There is no one simple solution to move teachers to accept fully that belief. For Beth, I realized it had happened when she stuck her head in the door one day and said, "Got a minute?"

I asked her to come in and sit down. Putting my elbows on the desk, I folded my hands, leaned forward, and began to listen as Beth described a situation in her classroom.

> The students have been writing personal narratives. We've participated in all these activities – things we talked about this summer – to involve the students in pre-writing exercises, so they connected with their writing before they wrote. After they wrote, I used some new tools I found in a writing book to push them to conference with their peers better and, I hope, to create better pieces. And, I've been looking at them. Of my 124 students there are still about 30 who are not 'writing proficient' (the standard students are expected to meet) in their personal narratives.

Beth was disappointed and exasperated, but I was thrilled. I leaned back in my chair and stopped her, "Listen to yourself," I said. "What's different about our conversation today?" Beth paused for a moment and thought. Suddenly a smile came over her face as she realized the difference.

"A year ago, I would not have cared if all the students accomplished proficiency. I would not have known to assess their progress and determine where they all were – to think about them as individuals," she stated with a bit of pride in her voice.

"You are exactly right," I confirmed. We took a few seconds to absorb the moment before trying to devise a game plan that would assist those 30 students in meeting proficiency. Soliciting other adult support for the students and meeting with our curriculum specialist to get more ideas emerged as steps to take.

All teachers can learn

This anecdote illustrates differentiated instruction for teachers. There are many teachers who are not ready for this type of discussion. There are others who have already made it to that point. For Beth, though, it was the right discussion at the right time. As her principal, I was interested in her classroom and professional growth. And it was my responsibility to talk with her individually about student improvement and student achievement.

There are also teachers caught in the middle. They are not bad teachers, but they have lost their drive to assertively hone their craft. They are satisfied with where they are. Most of them obediently attend school-level professional development. Some of them implement a few new ideas in their classrooms, while others put in their time just to get professional development credit. On professional development days, these teachers should not sit or work together. Negativity breeds negativity. With this in mind, I personally worked with a few teachers when assignments were given throughout the day. It is hard work, and it would be easier to sit in the back and ignore the teacher behavior. However, I always come back to the questions, "What if those teachers had my own child in their classroom?" and add "What would I want those teachers to know and be able to do?" Many answers came forward. Someone must believe in them, and who better than their principal?

Middle level principals who do not take steps to remove inadequate teachers from schools must also believe those teachers can improve. Principals must focus on believing, "If all **students can** learn, then all **teachers can** learn!" In professional development, we have the opportunity to serve each and every teacher.

Teachers are like students; they are all different and motivated by different learning conditions. They are at varying degrees of implementing sustained quality teaching and learning. Educators speak often about "differentiated instruction." Pushing this a bit further, what about "differentiated professional development"? All students are different, and all teachers are different, so a "one-size-fits-all" approach will not suffice.

Let's consider, then, how we can differentiate professional development for teachers. How can we view our faculties as we do our classrooms – a group of diverse learners? We need to take a proactive approach to building a learning community. This demands constant reflection about adult and student learning, and then taking action based on those reflections. Expressing expectations, assisting individuals who are unsuccessful, and then celebrating successes are appropriate actions. This type of learning community provides the foundation for teacher empowerment, student empowerment, and even parent empowerment. People need to hear the "You can do it" cheer inside their heads and thus be encouraged to step out and take risks. Helping others accept challenges also demands that the principal and staff are doing their own research and discovering cutting-edge practices. Once these practices are understood, the timing of introducing them becomes important.

ACTION STEPS

- Identify the superstar teachers in your school; then find ways that will challenge these excellent teachers to continue to grow professionally within your school culture. Seek their advice. Ask them to be mentors.

- Establish ways to help less accomplished teachers understand the expectation that every teacher needs to improve. Help them to get started on their improvement goals, and assign them a mentor, possibly their team leader.

- Think ahead to those teachers in your school who are caught in the middle. Determine ways that you can interact with them to nudge them toward improvement. Share copies of pertinent articles and websites.

TOPIC 2

An Overall Plan

In these days of school reform, schools can quickly find themselves making knee-jerk decisions from one test score to the next. It is important to identify and stick with a school vision, a school mission, and long-term goals. Too often, we jump on a new "save the day" reform program, and we skip from one purported panacea to another, from one year to the next. A better approach is to connect broader goals that take three to five years to accomplish. A Consolidated Planning Process can help focus on long-term goals and use financial and personnel resources appropriately. The process includes:

1. Collecting needs assessment data, including test scores, non-cognitive data, and student performance progress
2. Finding innovative practices that relate to recognized needs
3. Goal writing to identify short- and long-term goals
4. Identifying activities that meet the goals, including the use of technology, focused professional development, parent and community activities, and leadership activities
5. Using all funding for identified activities and goals
6. Establishing timelines that designate the completion of activities and establish a responsible stakeholder who ensures activities are sustained over time.

Typically, plans last two years before major revisions are needed. Collecting student work associated with the activities planned over time is important. This forces a faculty to validate its actions with results. It heightens the awareness that no one is just a hamster on a wheel, haphazardly spending funds. All actions are purposeful, and that purpose is student and adult growth around an understanding of what students should know and be able to do. The Consolidated Plan provides a vehicle for school leaders and schools as a whole to stay focused and say, "This is where we decided to go." The next step is looking to school community member actions to provide a means of getting there.

ACTION STEPS

◆ Create an action plan of communication to ensure that teachers, parents, and community members understand the school's long-term plan.

◆ Establish, if they do not exist, school procedures that ensure spending is consolidated and focused. Create policies that underpin efforts to make sure funding is spent on efforts to carry out the school's plan.

◆ Lead your school's stakeholders in integrating professional development opportunities within the school's improvement plan. Help them consider how these opportunities will impact instruction in the long term.

◆ Establish a system to ensure proper monitoring by school community members of the long-range plan. Use changes in teacher behavior and student improvement data as benchmarks for success.

Individual Growth Plans for teachers

A teacher's Individual Growth Plan should, of course, be linked with the school's long-term plan. It guides teachers' actions towards meeting both school and personal goals for improvement. When I first became a principal, I saw these forms as another thing I had to do. Teachers saw them the same way. Our school district required the forms to be completed annually, so teachers would get together and fill them out. They turned them into the school secretary, and we checked off that they had been done. I confess I used to say I did not have time to go over the Individual Growth Plans with teachers.

School Year _____

_____ Growth
_____ Assistive
_____ Corrective

Barren County Schools
Individual Professional Growth Plan

At least one growth activity will connect to the school's Consolidated Plan and one will connect to the individual's evaluation.

Evaluatee	Date	Work Site

A. Standard(s) I am working to achieve

B. What do I want to do, to meet the standard(s)?   How often/when will I do it?

C. How will I know what I did impacted student achievement?   Target Date(s)

D. Evaluatee's Comments	E. Evaluator's Comments

Individual Professional Growth Plan Developed	Achieved/Continued_____
_____ Evaluatee/Date	_____ Evaluatee/Date
_____ Evaluatee/Date	_____ Evaluatee/Date

I soon realized how Individual Growth Plans could provide needed momentum for achieving differentiated professional development. Completing the plan became a part of every teacher's last evaluation conference. The teachers who were not being formally evaluated on this yearly cycle completed theirs by May 1. They could carry a growth plan forward to the next year if they had not yet mastered what they were working on during that year. After holding discussions with teachers regarding their growth plans, the vice principal and I used a general consensus of teacher needs to assist our school's existing professional development committee. The committee then developed a schedule of school professional development offerings that supported the goals of the Consolidated Plan. These offerings included school-wide sessions, individual sessions, and attending state, regional, and national conferences.

After I became Director of Secondary Instruction, Individual Growth Plans became guides for the building level curriculum specialists as they worked with individual teachers. When the curriculum specialist and the evaluators understood the individual growth needs of each teacher, the system of assistance and evaluation worked in concert for professional improvement. Each of us held discussions with every teacher at different times, often on a weekly basis, in different contexts. For me, these contexts included times when I walked through school, in meetings where we looked at student work, and when we were formally participating in the evaluation cycle. At first, many teachers were not sure about my wanting to have a keen sense of the teaching methods they used. They preferred to close their doors and teach as they had been teaching, and they did not want a principal to push them to move to a higher level. Many of them had never had a principal who really wanted to know what students were learning, and they were skeptical about my motives.

To deal with this initial attitude of some, I focused on the students. As I walked through the school, we talked about specific students' strengths or what other students needed to experience success. This type of transition helped teachers see that our conversations occurred because I cared about them as professionals; I cared about their success with students; and I cared about the students' successes. Principals who walk the talk can accomplish the "can do" spirit associated with constant improvement.

ACTION STEPS

◆ Develop a personal vision for changing each and every teacher's behavior to help each and every student meet your state standards. Write your thoughts down, reflect on them, and finally write the vision on a card and place it where you'll occasionally see it.

◆ Take time to "play out" conversations in your mind, articulating thoughts that will create thinking opportunities for your teachers. Use these conversations to help teachers understand that you see them as individuals.

◆ Decide on two specific actions you will take in the next month to assist your "high-flying" teachers with their growth. Consider having two or three take the lead in presenting to the faculty their "best practices."

◆ Create your own action steps to work with teachers in your school who you think will not change. Decide on a specific action you can take to help them believe they can improve.

Focusing on the students

One easy way to focus on students is with Lauren Resnick's *Pittsburgh Walk-Through Process* (1998). This process offers instructional leaders a means of focusing on instruction as they move through the building. The focus is on students and learning. Teachers should recognize that such visits are not to evaluate them. Resnick has several standards she says are important to provide the optimum climate for student achievement. Of the many, two important ones are *Organized for Effort* and *Clear Expectations*. Each standard has questions for students that will determine how well the school has accomplished a climate for improvement. Based on the school's Consolidated Plan, the focus can be on the questions associated with Clear Expectations if it is determined that students need to better understand why they are learning the content.

Walking through the building and into classrooms, an administrator stops and asks students four questions, sometimes recording their responses. Four questions that focus on clear expectations are:

1. What are you learning?
2. Why are you learning it?
3. Is your work good?
4. How do you know it is good?

These four questions help an instructional leader understand how well teachers help students understand standards and the expectations associated with rubrics and scoring guides. Questions 1 and 3 are typically on target, but questions 2 and 4 tell the real story. For question 2, you would hope you would not hear students say, "Because the teacher said to," or "Because it's in the book."

Instead, one would like to hear, "We are learning X to be able to do Y." For question number 4, one would not want to hear students simply say their work was good, they worked hard, or got good grades. A more appropriate answer would relate to the rubric or scoring guide and why they thought their work fit a category within the scoring guide. When students can articulate that, they understand what they need to know and need to be able to do to perform the task.

The walk-through questions provide an opportunity for focusing on instruction and what students are learning as the principal moves through the school. They help the principal step back from classroom activity that looks good to gain a deeper understanding of the learning that occurs in classrooms. Using the questions does not mean that one could not talk with teachers or students about other things, but it does ensure that time is spent efficiently and focuses on instruction. Having completed a walk-through, it is desirable to send an E-mail to people where good things are occurring in their classrooms. Sometimes an E-mail can be sent to the entire faculty and staff just to provide encouragement and cheerlead risk taking a bit. It is not expected that administrators would use the full walk-through process every time they are moving about the building. Sometimes one might just ask students a single question, and other times one might have a brief exchange with the teacher.

How do walk-through questions help the leader to differentiate staff development? The process itself allows one to gain an understanding of individual classrooms; but the differentiation comes from what one does with the information. The answers to the questions are another source of data that can be used to develop thumbnail sketches of each teacher, what his/her improvement needs are, and where he/she is going, as these teachers seek to teach each and every student in their classrooms.

ACTION STEPS

◆ Develop your own system for moving through your school with an instructional focus and put it into practice this week. Block out different times on your calendar, three or four hours a week, for walk-throughs,

◆ Clarify the purpose behind spending time looking at student work, then sit in when a team is reviewing student work.

◆ In an upcoming faculty meeting, make student work the focus; perhaps have a team simulate one of its meetings and follow that demonstration with discussion.

TOPIC 3

Which Comes First, the Manager or the Leader?

In conference after conference and meeting after meeting, *instructional leadership* is espoused as a crucial key to meeting the standards in school reform. If we agree with this priority, the question "What does this really mean?" has to be faced. One thing is that we must first be able to manage so that we can lead. If we could successfully delineate the role so that the principal could be the chief executive officer in a middle school, and hire a business manager to manage the operational issues, we would not have to manage so that we could lead. Realistically, this will not happen, although experiments to provide such dual administrators were conducted many years ago, but never caught on. However, the role can and should be structured to limit the managerial tasks, utilizing other staff persons as appropriate.

High-performing schools are led by high-performing principals. High-performing principals know where to put their energies. There

---

What is the Principal's Most Important Role?

In a national Delphi Study the 59 characteristics of exemplary middle level principals, identified by an expert panel, were categorized into six roles: The exemplary middle school principal as

- a person
- a visionary
- an instructional leader
- a leader in an educational organization
- a manager
- a school community facilitator

The role of an instructional leader received the highest ranking, with the role of a visionary closely behind.

Source: *How To Become an Exemplary Middle School Principal: A Three-Step Professional Growth Handbook*, by Augustus Little and Suzanne Little (2001), National Middle School Association.

---

are many documents and studies that help us know what the priorities should be, and most principals have attended some type of training on instructional leadership. However, in daily practice, it is difficult to employ what we know we should be doing. Why?

One reason is what is sometimes called the "microwave mentality." In our world of E-mail, voice mail, faxes, FedEx, and microwaves, we want things to happen immediately. We are not patient enough to wait for snail mail, much less a change in culture or climate. Consequently, we struggle to focus on those actions that will lead to long-term success but require time-consuming changes in attitudes and culture. We mend wounds and create what we hope are quick cultural fixes daily. We often allow ourselves to spend precious hours disciplining students. These students almost universally come from teachers who do not have engaging classrooms and who do not know how to relate to students. We also spend time with parents and bus drivers discussing discipline issues. Instead of strategically thinking about needed education and implementation needs, we are like hamsters on wheels, spinning our way through a traditional school day, assigning alternative classroom time to students, trying to make decisions about student retention, or reacting to the next crisis that comes along.

Managing to lead

Let's think about an alternative that will permit us to guide and assist teachers in improving their classrooms. The question is, *How can we manage so that we can lead?* First, we must invest time and effort in hiring quality support staff who can deal with the minor events of the principalship. When I was first hired as an assistant principal and was trying to decide how and when to use the office assistants, the principal said to me, "If it doesn't take an administrative license to do it, you shouldn't be doing it." So, I got better at organizing tasks for the support staff to complete. We held bi-weekly staff meetings and invited the head custodian, the cafeteria manager, all the office support staff, andt he school administrative team. At these meetings, we organized for the upcoming events. If visitors were coming, we delegated who would order food, who would set up coffee, who would assemble information packets about the school, and who would greet visitors when they arrived. If a testing situation was coming up, we divided responsibilities associated with testing. This was a time to get organized so that the principal did not have to focus on the many managerial tasks in running a school.

The other key to successful staff meetings is having quality people at every position. Secretaries should be able to troubleshoot and solve problems. They need to be adept with technology, and if they do not know how to use a piece of software they should be willing to learn. The head custodian should be trained in building maintenance and should accept the premise that the presentation of the building supports high expectations. The cafeteria manager should be open to changing lunch schedules to meet the needs of students and be aware of the bigger picture outside the lunch schedule. Classified staff should see themselves as an important part of the entire school community. When their strengths are honored, and they are expected to grow as individuals, the principal can be the leader, the keeper of the vision, while others accomplish many of the managerial tasks.

Using the administrative team

An instructional leader uses the administrative team effectively and efficiently. For the middle level principal, there is always the danger that management issues are allowed to consume time needed for instructional leadership. To deal with this, responsibilities should be divided among the staff available, such as assistant principal, curriculum specialist, and guidance counselor so that each person has his/her own area of expertise. The *Interstate School Leadership Licensure Consortium Standards for School Leaders* (1996) makes it clear what a principal should be doing. The standards are clustered in the following six categories:

- Vision
- Teaching and Learning
- Management
- Community Involvement
- Ethical Behavior
- External Influences

Among these standards, *keeping the vision, teaching and learning, community relationships*, and *dealing with external influences* are the foundation for creating a quality teaching and learning environment. For the principal, this means focusing work daily on the following:

- Classroom walk-throughs, observations, and teacher evaluations linked to individualized professional development.
- Supporting curriculum work through daily conversations with teachers and consistent close work with the curriculum specialist or lead teacher.
- Ongoing and consistent parent communications
- Public relations activities including outside communications, grant writing, and working with other schools within and outside the district
- Community relations and supporting school-business partner-ships

While the principal focuses on these things, the assistant principal should handle discipline and oversee student services in the school. Such tasks as coordinating student attendance, managing the Exceptional Education Admissions and Release Committee meetings, and managing awards assemblies were delegated to the assistant principal. Of course, when needed, the principal should be involved, but the assistant principal can take care of student issues so that the principal can focus on teachers' professional growth needs. This makes it possible to hold more individual conversations with teachers. These one-on-one conversations are opportunities to nudge specific teachers toward the next level.

The school counselor can also be a significant player in the administrative organization. To accomplish this, the principal must work to prevent paperwork overload so the counselor can keep appointments with students, lead classroom preventive guidance sessions, facilitate a peer mediation program, and proactively counsel students based on their discipline and/or classroom performance. Within the administrative team, the counselor can also provide a strong voice for students by advocating for preventing student negativity before it starts. This provides the foundation for a positive school culture and for students who believe they can accomplish anything. This unique focus by the counselor keeps a positive school culture at the forefront of decision making, yet it allows the principal to focus on a larger picture than this one aspect of school culture.

Another critical member of the administrative team is the curriculum coordinator or specialist. While an administrative certification is usually not required for this position, the specialist at Barren county Middle School always met with the administrative team because she worked closely with teachers on job-embedded professional development. This role can be a strong impetus for change in classroom practice if used correctly. Teacher evaluations should guide the work of the curriculum specialist or the staff developer. During evaluation conferences, and even on a daily basis, school administrators observe teacher pedagogy that needs improvement. Where needed improvement is observed, the teacher evaluator should hold individual conversations with teachers in the hallways, classrooms, or offices. The tone of these conversations will be differentiated as well. Some teachers are motivated to change through lighthearted discussions; others will not respond if approached in this manner. Some teachers are threatened when they are asked to come to the office; others come on their own.

Keeping this in mind, deliberate decisions regarding when, where, and how to hold the conferences should be made. While principals want teachers to understand expectations for continuous improvement, they can also empower and support them as well.

At the close of teacher conversations, the curriculum specialist should be brought into the improvement cycle. The curriculum specialist is a resource teachers can use in their own improvement. The curriculum specialist can also model innovative practices in classrooms, hold discussions around quality instruction in team meetings, and help new teachers understand instructional practices that are significant practices within the school culture. Each action by the specialist should focus on the individual needs of the teacher with whom she is working as an important liaison between administration and teachers regarding professional growth. This person is usually not involved in evaluating teachers, and he/she can be an invaluable resource for teachers who are trying to improve their practice.

ACTION STEPS

◆ Take time to write out a list of activities you complete every day that are primarily managerial tasks. Reflect on them, and consider whether others could and should do some of them.

◆ In conferences, realign the duties of your administrative staff so that you empower them while allowing yourself time to focus on instruction and teacher development.

◆ Determine what motivates each teacher and how you will motivate each one.

◆ Consider the ways the curriculum specialist has been used and how this person could be used more effectively in improving teachers' instruction.

Growing leadership

As a middle level principal thinks about differentiated staff development, it is important to focus on the potential leadership already present in the school. With an administrator shortage pending and current low levels of teacher retention over time, principals have a responsibility to grow leaders while, at the same time, providing support and encouragement to the strong teachers they already have. Within the middle level structure, there are many opportunities for leadership development outside of the administrative team. The most obvious opportunity involves team leaders. Modeling instructional leadership and teaching team leaders how to be instructional leaders within their teams is difficult, but productive. The reality of the principalship makes it impossible to meet with teams for instructional planning all the time; therefore, developing team leaders' understanding of interdisciplinary instruction and a cohesiveness in instruction among the team is a must. The tenure of team leaders has to be considered. Team leaders do not have to continue their position more than one year, but there is merit in continuity. What is best for the team's growth is the primary consideration. When someone fulfills the role more than two years, something of a "seniority position" is created in the school culture. There are many nuances attached to selecting team leaders that have to be recognized.

Principals can begin the year with a one- or two-day team leader training where the more routine administrative roles of the team leaders are de-emphasized and the more professional role of instructional leadership is emphasized. The agenda for these sessions should not only provide concrete examples of how to keep team members focused on instruction, but also provide needed opportunities for team leaders to become a team themselves.

Collectively, team leaders are on the front line where change has to occur; they serve as a sounding board regarding the pace of change. At team leader meetings, whole school improvement issues are discussed, and heartaches regarding the change process are shared, while confidentiality is honored. The principal can also use his/her understanding of team members' comfort levels regarding change to measure the pulse of the school and everyone's comfort level or readiness regarding the change at hand.

Monthly team leader meetings, with intentionally planned agendas, follow the summer meeting. By keeping the "management issues" off the table to the greatest extent possible, the principal can hold true to an agenda that focuses on classroom and team improvement. This ultimately results in better opportunities for middle level students to improve their learning. Teachers want their team leader to run interference with administration. All individual questions and concerns can quickly come to the principal due to the high accessibility E-mail provides. Team leader meetings should be reserved for group problem solving, with team leaders bringing team success stories along with concerns. And, anyone who brings a concern must also bring a possible solution to start the problem-solving discussion. This is an important feature that keeps meetings from becoming gripe sessions.

Throughout the years, many Barren County teachers grew professionally. Two recent Kentucky Middle School Teachers of the Year hailed from the school. Others have secured or are seeking school administration positions. There are other examples to confirm the fact that leaders can be home grown. As teachers are encouraged to step up, they grow confident in their leadership abilities, and they are willing to explore new opportunities for themselves, their schools, and for the education community.

ACTION STEPS

◆ Develop and implement a plan that will encourage leaders to emerge within the school.

◆ Become conscious of how your discussions with individual teachers will cause the best teachers to aspire to be leaders, and others will commit to making improvements.

◆ Copy a recent article on curriculum integration and place it in a team leader's box with a note asking the team leader to share it at the next team leaders' meeting.

◆ Start making plans for a team leaders' training session prior to the opening of school next year. Consider inviting a successful team leader from another system to serve as a resource person.

◆ Have team leaders carefully examine copies of National Middle School Association's *Staff Development Kit #3, Revitalizing Teaming to Increase Achievement* and Middle Level Leadership Series *Taking Teaming to the Next Level: The Principal's Role* (see p. 42) to determine how these resources may be used.

◆ Put all team leaders and related personnel on a group E-mail address to encourage regular communication with these individuals between monthly meetings.

TOPIC 4

Improving Instruction
Through Professional Development Strategies

Looking at student work

One of the most useful strategies principals can employ to increase student learning and achievement is to encourage teachers to look at and analyze student work. Team sessions where teachers discuss student work, its relation to standards, and the changes that teachers can make to improve the quality of student work should be a regular part of each team's agenda. Quite often this work is organized in content areas, and each content area should select its leader once a year. Since many team leaders already receive a stipend, one has to be creative in compensating teachers for accepting this new content leader role.

Members of the administrative team – assistant principal, guidance counselor, curriculum specialist, or principal – should work with a specific content area throughout the school year based on their strengths. The administrator should not lead discussions in content leader meetings but should clarify information when needed. Also, at the beginning of the year, a training session should be held for content leaders. This session will focus on honing content leaders' facilitation skills and will emphasize student learning and teacher pedagogy. Content teachers must be committed to this work if the process is beneficial, ultimately leading to higher student achievement

To facilitate the process of examining student work, teachers should keep monthly work samples from the same students representing low, medium, and high-achieving students. When teachers meet quarterly in their content areas, they examine these student work samples to determine if students are consistently learning the material and if they are able to communicate about that content through writing at a proficient level. Furthermore, teachers discuss instructional strategies that will assist all students in improving their thinking and writing. Content leaders are critical to success when looking at student work.

When schools begin this process, they usually can say where the students are, but they have not typically examined individual teacher practices to determine if they are, in fact, preventing learning or assisting at-risk learners. Classroom practices that create opportunities for high level students to soar have not been identified either. However, as teachers continue looking at student work, conversations will lead to examining teacher practices that challenge all levels of learners.

Content meetings are also used to analyze and interpret test data. Teachers dissect subgroup data and discuss reasons for student success or lack of success. These discussions also lead to creating activities for a school's long-term consolidated or improvement plan.

Though not usually labeled professional development sessions, content meetings for examining student work become just that. After teachers become more comfortable with the organization of the meetings, they begin to share more openly with one another as they do in their team meetings. They share "tricks of the trade," success stories, and try to determine how to help each and every student. These sessions in themselves provide a means of differentiated instruction for teachers. Those who are comfortable bring their issues to the table, and at times, the issues are the same across content areas. When this happens, the school leadership should address them in a more comprehensive manner. Other times, the issues are very different, and teachers help one another find solutions. In any case, if a school has a School-Based Decision-Making Council, by whatever name, the council should review reports from content meetings to discern common problems or issues across the school that need to be dealt with as a total school.

◆   Set specific monthly meetings for content areas to look at student work.

◆   Develop a plan to coordinate the work of interdisciplinary teams with the content area activities. How will the work of both groups support understanding student achievement?

Attending state, regional, and national conferences

An excellent means for advancing professional development is sending teachers to major conferences, especially national conferences. Such conferences provide rich experiences that cannot be provided any other way. If the school budget will allow, send as many teachers as you can. A professional conference can be the spark for a teacher to re-energize, just as it can benefit a teacher who would like to attend every year. Attending national conferences should become a budget item in the school's consolidated plan, and parameters should be established to determine who attends.

Establish priorities for which teachers should attend based on current school priorities. For example, teachers whose primary responsibility is in the content area of the upcoming textbook adoption should have priority to attend a national conference of their choice. Allow different grade level teachers to attend, perhaps sending intact teams or subgroups of teams across grade levels.

Finally, if a teacher is accepted as a presenter at a conference, funds should be located for him or her to attend, as this is professional development itself. Most of the time, an administrator should accompany the group. Ensuring that the wealth of information gained by attending is shared is important and requires planning and follow up. Team meetings and content area meetings are platforms for sharing discussion. An entire faculty meeting may be used for reports on conferences, but this is never sufficient in and of itself. Teachers who attend may be required to fill out a form before they go, telling how they will share information when they return. The principal should establish the expectation that attendees will share in ways that teachers can be affected by the knowledge gained and have a chance to internalize and use the information the conference attendees gained.

ACTION STEPS

◆ Principals should be professionally active! Attend meetings, read and share journals, and attend conferences and workshops. This is essential.

◆ Have your teachers present to the board of education anytime someone attends a conference. This will demonstrate the great value of attending conferences and give examples to show that it is money well spent and why it should be a regularly budgeted item.

◆ Create procedures in your school that ensure knowledge gained at conferences will be shared, understood by other faculty members, and implemented.

◆ Demonstrate to teachers that you value conference attendance as a means of remaining on the cutting edge of classroom practices. Be a vocal advocate for promising practices.

◆ Use national conference attendance as a means of differentiating professional development for all levels of teachers.

◆ Encourage a teacher or a team to apply to present at the next National Middle School Association conference. Provide the form needed.

Professional development activities for the entire staff

With a commitment to differentiating conversations and necessary teacher activities, there are also some professional development events in which the entire staff should participate. These events help accomplish long-term school goals, and they usually center around specific changes in teacher pedagogy. According to Robert Marzano (2000), teachers on a team should use a common vocabulary with the students they teach. This helps students "hear" better and remember concepts longer. With this in mind, principals who want a whole faculty to use a common vocabulary should afford them common professional development experiences prior to the opening of school. During these few days, the principal should be the lead learner, either as presenter or active participant. Alongside this active involvement, the principal can observe how well the teachers are internalizing the information and how comfortable they appear to be with the concepts. The instructional leader can then use this information to guide discussions with teachers at varying degrees of complexity.

Observing teachers at professional development events can provide cues for a principal's conversations with teachers throughout the year. Noting body language, questions they ask, and comments made to colleagues also help the administrative team determine the type of follow-up needed. Avoiding a "one-size-fits-all" approach, the principal can began with one type of delivery and end with differentiated guidance for teachers.

One such way to differentiate guidance for teachers is by visits to schools where best practices are implemented. As a part of continuous improvement, the school can seek out schools within the state or region that emulate quality middle level practices with high performance on assessment and accountability. Once the schools to visit are identified, based on your school's professional development needs, the principal can choose who makes the visits in light of the growth needs of teachers.

ACTION STEPS

◆ Assess anew the most recent professional development program. Did it provide a common school-wide focus in support of the school's mission?

- Plan the next program to ensure an adequate common focus from which differentiated follow-ups can evolve.
- Confer with in-school and district level personnel responsible for staff development to reach consensus on the need for common and differentiated experiences and how both responsibilities can be met using coaching, job-embedded staff development, attending conferences, and leadership opportunities.
- Establish a list of high-performing middle schools in your state that your staff members can visit. Decide today which school you will visit first and what teachers will go.

The academy approach

Once teachers learn about interdisciplinary instruction and integrated learning at the middle level, there is still a need to ratchet up content, yet keep middle level pedagogy viable. Teachers will ask for "content-based" professional development, and principals should emphasize connecting content through interdisciplinary instruction.

This is where the "academy approach" enters the picture. Academies are a type of study group, or a Critical Friends approach to staff development. They create a community of learners, a group of teachers who can learn more by collaborating. A word of caution about establishing academies! It is hard and time-consuming work. However, the professional morale and benefits can be enormous when you design what is, in effect, a miniature long-term conference for teachers. If you have a small school, work with your local high school or with other middle schools in your area. Consider these suggestions when establishing an academy.

1. The academy should follow the standards of the National Staff Development Council (1999) regarding up-front class time, job-embedded learning, an understanding of who to ask for help in implementing, and timely follow-up.

2. Use a needs assessment to identify the school's long-term improvement plan, and/or teacher surveys to identify the pedagogical needs of your teachers around standards-based teaching and learning. What do teachers need to improve their implementation of varied teaching and learning practices? What do they need to understand so they can help all students learn? The answers to these questions will be different for different teachers; however, common themes will occur, and these needs can be the focus of the first academies.

3. Establish a format for the academy. The hardest part is to find a specific time for follow-up and teacher reflection. One format consists of two days in a summer workshop, a half-day follow up in the fall, and a half-day follow-up in the spring. Different academy groups establish when their half days will be; this gives some ownership in choosing the dates through the school year. Care should be taken to choose dates in the summer when teachers can attend. Ask them!

4. Establish an electronic component to the learning whereby teachers can communicate with their peers throughout the year. Typically, teachers won't send or respond to an E-mail unless they are trying to implement a strategy or solve a problem with their students. When they do write in, they have a group of peers to respond to their needs. This is timely, job-embedded follow-up to their own professional development. If someone is willing to post questions to facilitate the listserv and keep the discussion going, a strong learning community can develop. A school or school district can set up groups of people to chat in several ways. The easiest way to set up the groups is by just asking participants to click "Reply to All" when they finish composing their E-mail. However, if there is strong technology support within the school or district, the person responsible for technology can set up the groups into listserv format.

5. Recruit facilitators for the professional learning experience, possibly someone within your faculty or from the district office. In some school cultures, it is more effective to use someone from within, saving travel expenses. In other cultures, the learning will occur best if someone from outside the district is the facilitator. Either way, the facilitator is the person who leads the initial staff development days, facilitates the reflective discussions in the fall and the spring around student products that demonstrate implementation of new learning in the previous summer, and is the discussion leader on the listserv. It is important to establish this in the contract, up front, because this is a different way of accomplishing professional development, and presenters might not expect to do more than what they normally do in a workshop. The presenters should be compensated for the planning, teaching, and related work.

6. Determine a place to host the academy that is *learning friendly* with tables for working, and food and drinks available.

7. Advertise the opportunities to staff and ask people to sign up for the academy of their choice, based on their own learning needs.

8. Meet with the facilitators about a month prior to the first days of this experience. This meeting will elevate the success of the experience for teachers and is a must in the planning stage. No one knows teachers' professional growth needs better than a principal. As the instructional leader, set expectations for the facilitators, based on the participants' needs. Do not allow the facilitators to just present the information. Instead, help them to mesh their strong teaching skills with the needs of the teachers attending the academy. Establish the necessity of developing a genuine learning community, and plan times where participants share their expertise.

9. Outline requirements with the facilitators for teachers to share student products throughout the year that demonstrate the teacher is implementing what they are learning within their classrooms. When the academies reconvene, participants can examine this student work to determine if new teacher practices are positively affecting student progress.

10. Since there will be several academies, and they are multi-day approaches, it will not be feasible for the middle level principal to attend all sessions. Knowing that, it is important for the middle level leader to spend significant time when the academies are being planned. Have conversations with individual teachers prior to the first days of the experience; help them think about how their participation in the academy will serve their needs.

11. Throughout the year, talk with individual teachers about the work they are doing in the academy.

ACTION STEPS

◆ What forms of faculty study groups currently exist? Are they effective as a means of ongoing staff development?

◆ Pull together an ad hoc committee to consider establishing academies. Set a timeline for initiating academies following a full examination and approval of the idea.

◆ Individualize follow-up activities for varying levels of teacher learning.

◆ While the focus of the academies is on improved curriculum and instruction, make sure that the foundational nature and developmental needs of young adolescents are not overlooked.

Creating time for conversations

Tom Peterson, former Associate Commissioner in the Kentucky Department of Education, believes conversations are what truly change practice. His point is well taken; so with this in mind, the middle level leader must create opportunities for informal, professional conversations to occur and a climate that fosters such. Academies, content meetings, and team meetings, when structured correctly, are obvious opportunities. Informal conversations when walking around provide the leader with the chance to conduct what Lounsbury (1991) has labeled "wayside teaching," ... "the teaching that is done between classes, when walking in the halls, after school, and in dozens and dozens of one-on-one encounters, however brief. For principals it is usually the main means of teaching" (p. 29). There are other times in the school day that conversations can occur, lunch, for instance. Ongoing conversations – in a natural sense – promote continuous teacher improvement and continuous teacher change toward classroom pedagogy that leads to success for all students.

ACTION STEPS

◆ Initiate conversations with your teachers about the level of student learning occurring in their classrooms to establish the importance of improving classroom practice.

◆ If you have a faculty lounge, solicit the help of a small faculty committee to rearrange or redecorate. Stock with journals, monographs, and books. Put up a bulletin board focused on such professional issues as standards for student learning or assessment examples and get people to talk about these things. Arrange for new items to be added regularly and old ones removed.

◆ When you see a teacher conducting a very effective activity, ask that teacher to share it with a teacher you think could learn from it.

Finding a way to fund it

Administrators are now saying to themselves, "All this sounds great, but how do you pay for it?" Funding multiple professional development opportunities can be accomplished as long as these opportunities hold a priority within the school, and better yet, district budgets. And, as a leader you can help to establish that priority. The school and district leadership must hold staff development important enough to warrant funds.

To begin, one should understand that many categorical funds have an allowable percentage of that money for the development of teachers. The *No Child Left Behind* law provides multiple sources for this, including Title I, Title II, and Title V funds; however those same funds can be used for other objectives as well. The National Middle School Association's Middle Level Leadership Series, *No Child Left Behind: Implications for Middle Level Leaders* by Patricia George (2002), provides information on the many funding opportunities within the new law.

Beyond the federal funding streams, there are state funding streams as well. Typically, schools receive some state funds for professional development, and these funds should be maximized within the total budget – another reason to keep professional development as a top priority in the school's Consolidated Plan. If the specific development funds are not enough, local funds should be used. The bottom line is that quality professional development presented at varied teacher levels will create long-term success for the educator and the students by ultimately changing teacher pedagogy for the better. Continuous professional development with focus, individualized follow-through, and expectations for implementation is the long-term solution for improvement in our schools and classrooms.

The challenge is on the middle level principal to educate school stakeholders regarding the value of quality professional development and integrate follow-up into the daily routines of the school. And, finally, the onus is on stakeholders to create and support a menu of professional development, a diversified portfolio so to speak, that will serve the individual needs of all the staff members while providing some common growth areas as well.

ACTION STEPS

◆. Maintain a presence of staff development in your school's long-term plans while remembering that school improvement will not come without a cost.

◆ Highlight results of various staff development experiences in newsletters and announce at faculty meetings .

◆ Maintain a comprehensive approach to spending your staff development funds so that they are spent according to your school improvement goals

The rest of Becky's story

Becky Moon smiles now. Almost three years after I joined Barren County Middle School, I noticed Becky had changed. She often smiled. She talked with students – as opposed to yelling at them. There was activity as well as "learning noise" in her classroom. One day in the spring, I got up the nerve to ask Becky how the change had occurred.

"First," she said, "I knew that changing my classroom was important to you. I knew that you believed in the multiple intelligences, and it is important to me to do what is asked of me. I wasn't sure I agreed with you at the time, but I started because I knew it was important to you."

Becky then shared that once she started making changes, she needed to see a difference in students' learning according to *her* evaluation of student achievement. At the end of the first unit where she had involved her students in projects and in active classroom learning events, her students' grades were very good. (Throughout this time, I knew that Beth had been helping Becky, giving her ideas when she needed them and encouraging her when she was scared about taking a risk.) When Becky looked at the grades, she inferred that they were too high. So she decided to give her traditional test, authored by the textbook company, to lower the grades. Her experience told her that students never did well on those types of tests. She gave the test, and the grades were better than they had been in her 25 years of teaching! Becky was sold. She had taken a risk, changed her practice, and the change was validated. She began to take other risks because she believed she was making the right decisions for students.

Since then, Becky has become a proponent for teaching differently because today's students are different, and we know more about learning. In the year of her change in pedagogy, our school had been invited to present our successes at a national conference. We determined how many people we had funds to send and drew for those slots, since we had more who wanted to go than we could afford. Becky's name was chosen. The timing was right for her to attend a national conference. She came back stronger in her belief that we were on the right track. She had a newfound pride in what we were trying to accomplish and was more self-assured. Now, other principals in our district want Becky to talk with their faculties. Without differentiated professional development, I probably would have given up on Becky. Instead, when we began to see a glimmer of change, we capitalized on Becky's strengths and on her venturing out of her normal mode, one step at a time. Working with her was not a one-shot approach; it was multifaceted, just as it has to be when we want our students to grow. Now, Becky will tell visitors, "This is not fake. I really do teach and plan like this all the time!"

That's what differentiated professional development is all about!

Resources Relevant to Differentiating Staff Development

The *Middle Level Leadership Series* is designed for busy but committed middle level leaders. These relatively brief, to-the-point treatments of timely topics promote taking action. The two previous titles are apropos to this topic.

- *No Child Left Behind: Implications for Middle Level Leaders,* by Patricia George
- *Taking Teaming to the Next Level: The Principal's Role,* by Jerry Rottier

Safe To Be Smart: Building a Culture for Standards-Based Reform in the Middle Grades, by Anne Wheelock, takes the call for standards-based reform out of the political and upper-echelon educational arenas and into the classroom. Descriptions of successful practices give credence to this solid book's message – and the hope that real change is possible

Staff Development Kits are a form of homegrown professional development. With these kits-in-a-book, individual teachers, teams, or faculties can work their way through activities, often during common planning periods, to grow professionally and personally. All materials needed are included.

- *Kit #1: Implementing the Middle School Concept (Middle School 101)*
- *Kit #2: How to Improve Discussion and Questioning Practices: Tools and Techniques.*
- *Kit #3: Revitalizing Teaming to Improve Student Learning.*

This We Believe: Developmentally Responsive Middle Level Schools, National Middle School Association's foundation position paper, is recognized as the leading statement on the characteristics of effective middle schools. It provides the vision that should direct all plans for improvements. Every middle level educator should be familiar with it.

How to Become an Exemplary Middle School Principal: A Three-Step Professional Growth Handbook is a unique do-it-yourself resource that can help a principal examine and reorder the almost overwhelming responsibilities of leading an exemplary middle school.

Turning Points 2000: Educating Adolescents in the 21st Century is the critically important follow-up to the Carnegie Corporation's landmark 1989 *Turning Points*. Full treatments of curriculum, instruction, and assessment make this a "must have" for all middle level leaders.

For ordering information on the above NMSA publications, call 1-800-528-NMSA or visit NMSA's website at www.nmsa.org .

Additional Related Resources:

Blasé, J., & Blasé, J. ((1998). *Handbook of instructional leadership*. Thousand Oaks, CA: Corwin Press.

Bolman, L., & Deal, T. (1995). *Leading with soul*. San Franscisco. Jossey-Bass Publishers.

Buckingham, M., & Coffman, C. (1999). *First, break all the rules*. New York. Simon and Schuster.

Covey, S. R. (1990). *The seven habits of highly effective people*. New York. Simon and Schuster.

Gregory, G. H., & Chapman, C. (2002). *Differentiated instructional strategies*. Thousand Oaks, CA. Corwin Press.

References

George, P. (2002). *Middle Level leadership series. No child left behind: Implications for middle level leaders.* Westerville, OH: National Middle School Association.

Interstate School Leaders Licensure Consortium. (1996). *Standards for school leaders.* Washington, DC: Council of Chief State School Officers.

Little, A., & Little, S. (1991). *How to become an exemplary middle school principal: A three-step professional growth handbook.* Westerville, OH: National Middle School Association.

Lounsbury, J. H. (1991). *As I see it.* Columbus, OH: National Middle School Association.

Marzano, R. (2000). *What works in classroom instruction.* Aurora, CO. Mid-Continent Research for Education and Learning. Interstate School Leadership Consortium.

National Staff Development Council (1999). *Standards for staff development.* Author.

Resnick, L. (1998). *The Pittsburgh walk-through process.* Pittsburgh, PA. University of Pittsburgh.

National Middle School Association

National Middle School Association, established in 1973, is the voice for professionals and others interested in the education and well-being of young adolescents. The association has grown rapidly and enrolls members in all 50 states, the Canadian provinces, and 42 other nations. In addition, 57 state, regional, and provincial middle school associations are official affiliates of NMSA.

NMSA is the only national association dedicated exclusively to the education, development, and growth of young adolescents. Membership is open to all. While middle level teachers and administrators make up the bulk of the membership, central office personnel, college and university faculty, state department officials, other professionals, parents, and lay citizens are members and active in supporting our single mission – improving the educational experiences of 10-15 year olds.

This open and diverse membership is a particular strength of NMSA's. The association publishes *Middle School Journal,* the movement's premier professional journal; *Research in Middle Level Education Online; Middle Ground, the Magazine of Middle Level Education; Target,* the association's newsletter; *Family Connection,* an online newsletter for families; *Classroom Connections,* a practical quarterly resource; and a series of research summaries.

A leading publisher of professional books and monographs in the field of middle level education, NMSA provides resources both for understanding and advancing various aspects of the middle school concept and for assisting classroom teachers in planning for instruction. More than 70 NMSA publications are available through the resource catalog as well as selected titles published by other organizations.

The association's highly acclaimed annual conference has drawn many thousands of registrants every fall. NMSA also sponsors many other professional development opportunities.

For information about NMSA and its many services, contact the association's headquarters office at 4151 Executive Parkway, Suite 300, Westerville, Ohio, 43081. TELEPHONE: 800-528-NMSA; FAX: 614-895-4750; INTERNET: www. nmsa.org.